Move to learn

Move to learn

Caroline Scott

Published by
Speechmark Publishing Ltd, 70 Alston Drive,
Bradwell Abbey, Milton Keynes MK13 9HG, UK
Tel: +44 (0) 1908 326 944   Fax: +44 (0) 1908 326 960
www.speechmark.net

www.schoolofemotional-literacy.com

002-5460/Printed in the United Kingdom/1010

British Library Cataloguing in Publication Data

Scott, Caroline
  Move to learn
  1. Movement education 2. Children with mental disabilities
  - Education 3. Children with social disabilities -
  Education 4. Special education - Activity programmes
  I. Title
  371.9'043

ISBN 978 0 86388 684 3

Contents

Making the connection

This book starts with the premise that movement, particularly if it is specific and intentional, enhances learning.

From their earliest days, youngsters need to move around, to explore, experiment and interact with their environment. Sitting still can bring passivity, boredom and a lack of stimulation that is disabling. We need to use all our brain and integrate the information we hear through our ears, see through our eyes and touch with our bodies to make sense of the world. Movement can create new neural pathways to use this information and bring functionality, meaning and memory.

At first, virtually all learning takes place through movement as a baby begins to make spontaneous and then intentional movements. Movement provides information about their new world but very quickly children learn to sit still and become immobile, stiff and rigid. There are fewer opportunities in school to find out about the body, to roll on the floor, hang upside down, explore fast and slow movement, high and low shapes and to notice the differences between them.

The activities in *Move to Learn* are all about getting the brain ready for learning through movement, which increases the oxygen supply and arouses interest and alertness. Just look at the faces of children in a school hall during PE – feel the energy and sense the excitement. Exercises enliven the learning environment and bring back a sense of fun and enjoyment, creating a readiness for learning.

Research from neurophysiology tells us that simple movements help the development of the brain and enhance the communication between different parts of the brain. For example, Dennison (1989) talks about 'whole-brain learning' using intentional movement and particularly Brain Gym activities to enable students to use those parts of the brain previously inaccessible to them.

For children who are in emotional distress or upset during the school day, taking part in the movement sessions can punctuate a stressful situation in class and change the mood. It is hard to be anxious when relaxed, fearful when excited or angry when expending energy. Being physically active helps to dissipate the 'flight or fight' stress responses in the body and bring back emotional stability. Many children need a 'brain break' from intense concentration on academic tasks and sitting too long, immobile at a desk. The structured sessions can offer physical relief, refreshing the body and the brain so that children can return to their classroom learning in a more receptive frame of mind.

Movement, moreover, leads to self-awareness of the body and the body in space. Self-awareness is noticing whether our body is tense or relaxed, what our posture is like and whether our body is strong and fit enough to cope with the emotional demands of everyday life. It is about how happy we feel inside our body and our own sense of well-being – knowledge and understanding that lead to self-help and self-management. Children must feel comfortable and at home in their bodies. Ingun Schneider (2001) writes, 'If a child experiences his body as an ill-fitting glove, settling down and paying attention to the task at hand are very difficult'.

These ingredients contribute to the overall level of personal emotional 'literacy' that we experience and develop. When we are aware of our bodies, how they work and what they can do, we are more likely to have confidence in our actions and the ability to develop a better perception of ourselves. As we attain greater motor control, we are more likely to develop a sense of effectiveness in the world around us. Activities that help this intrapersonal understanding to grow, either using the whole body or focusing on specific parts, are vital to the way that we learn to support and nurture ourselves.

When we understand ourselves we can begin to act with self-management, changing those things that do not feel right and modifying how we respond to people and events around us. We are no longer at the mercy of our emotions telling us how we should react – we can stop and think, making a choice in our actions and selecting ways in which we can look after ourselves better. We can learn how to be calm and quiet, soothe ourselves and be peaceful in a turbulent world.

Move to Learn involves activities shared between an adult and a child or a small group of children. It is here that we can start to develop our interpersonal skills and our ability to build trusting relationships with others. Working together allows observation, comparison, knowledge, acceptance and celebration of other people. It enables children to develop and practise social interaction in a safe setting and to grow and nurture supportive friendships.

What's it all about?

Move to Learn **is a movement programme for children aged from five to eight years, delivered in sessions, working one-to-one with an adult or as a small group.**

You can choose a session just as you wish or plan a series as part of a pastoral programme or intervention in a school or similar setting. You can use the programme to liven up a day, provide a 'brain break' in the curriculum, or offer a complete change for a pupil who is having an emotionally challenging day. You can pick and choose from the activities to fill a 10 to 30 minute time slot.

Where the programme is planned in advance, it is envisaged that there would be six sessions running on consecutive weeks at the same time and in the same place, each lasting approximately 30 minutes. These sessions should be carefully and purposefully structured, each following a similar format. Ideally, they would be run to fit into a half-term period and might then be repeated or expanded with other children.

If you work with younger children you will need to adapt the instructions and offer lots of modelling and working together. Running the sessions with children and their parents can be especially rewarding and provide suggestions for activities to do at home.

The main aim of the programme is to get children moving. Moving promotes learning. Other outcomes will follow:

☐ **Emotional** – encouraging happy, secure, confident, motivated and positive emotional states in the limbic system of the brain to support a sense of well-being.

☐ **Cognitive** – using movement to create and strengthen neural pathways, to integrate brain activity and develop 'whole brain' learning.

☐ **Motor** – enabling children to develop their gross and fine motor skills; to understand being active or calm and to know the difference.

☐ **Social** – using activities to have fun and play together; to interact and build good relationships.

☐ **Language** – to encourage good listening skills and attending to instructions; to learn to use self-talk – the conversations we have in our heads that help to rehearse new knowledge and ideas and so mediate learning, and help to clarify our thoughts and feelings.

Menu of activities

The activities are arranged in nine sections to address different sorts of movement:

1. Stamina.
2. Large motor actions.
3. Mobility.
4. Balance.
5. Dexterity.
6. Spatial awareness.
7. Body awareness.
8. Fine motor skills.
9. Rhythm and sequence.
10. Relaxation.

Evaluation of the programme

You may wish to put in place an evaluation of the programme by using pre- and post-intervention data gathering and this might include some of the following:

- [ ] Asking the children for their views: see Appendix A.

- [ ] Collecting parents' views and general comments: see Appendix B.

- [ ] A teachers' questionnaire about changes in a pupil's behaviour: see Appendix C.

- [ ] A parents' questionnaire about changes in their child's behaviour: see Appendix D.

- [ ] Emotional Literacy Indicator: see Morris and Scott (2002).

Equipment inventory

Activities will be carried out in a large but confined space such as a small school hall or large meeting room.

Basic PE equipment will be needed for some activities such as bean bags, skittles, large and small balls, soft balls, hoops and mats.

Activities to develop fine motor skills will need a range of materials as detailed in that section.

Loose clothes and bare feet work best. PE kit is not needed.

Caution

Make sure children start by working within their physical limits and only gradually encourage a greater range and duration of movement. Actions should never be forced or cause muscle strain.

Working as a group

The groupwork sessions should be fun and enjoyable for all. It has been found that it takes time for children to settle to something that is new, and perhaps a little scary, when they are not sure what is going to happen. You may find that it is only after two or three sessions that the children calm down, trust what is going on and begin to engage purposefully.

It is well worth spending time to explain to children's parents and teachers what the aims are, what you hope to achieve and why you think it will be particularly valuable for the children who have been selected. Try to keep in touch and offer feedback about progress – steps forward and steps still to take. This is most effective when parents and teachers are looking out for positive changes and noticing what happens. You may need to take time to explain the aims and objectives again once the sessions have got going and there is more to talk about.

By taking part in the sessions, the children will inevitably miss what is going on in class, so it is crucial to have staff and parents 'on board' and backing the success of the group. The children may need opportunities to catch up on things they have missed and this will need to be factored into the planning.

Deciding who should be invited to join a group may be tricky. A scarce resource in a school is always in demand. It has been found that it helps to have children of similar age working together and that it works best in a group of four to six children, although there could be more if there is room and there are extra adults available to help. Clear reasons for joining or 'entry criteria' will make explanations to others easier.

A series of weekly sessions is likely to be planned, perhaps six or eight so that they fit into a half-term period and may then be repeated with other children. When the series comes to an end will probably decide the 'exit criteria', although other issues could be involved. A review at that time can decide whether further sessions would be beneficial.

I have run the sessions with children and their parents and this can give parents ideas for activities to try at home – particularly with young children – to help them interact and have fun together.

Although a series of sessions is likely to be planned, an adult might also work with a 'child in crisis' using a session spontaneously. The activities could provide a complete change or distraction, a 'brain break', or an opportunity to release some energy or practise relaxation. Suitable activities could be chosen from the menu to help a child cope successfully through the school day.

Running structured sessions

Planned weekly sessions are likely to work best when the same room is available on the same day and at the same time. It is important to be ready with equipment and all the resources so that everything is at hand and sessions can start promptly. When a school hall is used, the children will want to run around and use the space. But it is also important to be able to create a cosy, small-group space, particularly for the closing section.

The first part of the session lasts about five minutes and is called **Hello and welcome!** This is a time to welcome everyone and to develop a sense of belonging and inclusion for the group. The first few minutes set the scene, so make sure everyone is comfortable and tuned in. Activities here are used to introduce participants to each other, to learn everyone's name and to relax, as children may be feeling tense and apprehensive. It is a chance to focus and introduce what should be a positive learning experience.

Aims	Format	Activities
Hello and welcome: *'We're glad you're here and we value what you bring.'*	Sitting on the floor in a circle.	Ice-breakers: Circle Time and social inclusion games such as roll a ball across the circle to a friend saying, *'Hello, I'm Ben'*, or *'Pass the squeeze or smile'*.

The session will flow into a period of greater activity lasting about five to ten minutes and called **Getting going.**

Now is the time to be active, expend some energy and use the whole body. Activities here are likely to need a large but confined space so that children do not run off and your instructions can be heard. Children can increase their heart rate, develop physical stamina and understand what it feels like to be in motion. Encourage large and fast actions but also contrast these with slow ones.

Aims	Format	Activities
Warm-up exercises and activities to develop stamina such as *'I can move my whole body. I can keep going for ages'*.	Large but confined space.	Moving the whole body, large actions and keeping going: for example star jumps, skipping around the room, throwing bean bags.

Stop and pause is the next part and will again last for about five to ten minutes. It is designed to involve more controlled and quieter activities, to allow the child to become more aware of his or her body and its intricate movements. This may involve a large communal space and individual space.

Aims	Format	Activities
Activities to develop concentration, attention and stillness: *'I can do quiet, gentle movement. I can find out about myself.'*	Sitting or standing as a group. Also providing some opportunities for travelling around a small space.	*Slow, careful movements such as standing and lowering the body to a crouch position, rocking from heels to toes, rotating wrists and clapping sequences.*

The session ends with a 'wind down' or calming period: **Peace at last.** Here children can learn new skills to calm themselves, to undergo relaxation sequences and be peaceful – skills for life that are often hard to acquire and put in place.

Aims	Format	Activities
To learn how to relax: *'I can be quiet, still and at peace.'*	Sitting/lying in a large space or grouped close together.	Movements that promote relaxation of the muscles and a quiet state of mind, such as systematic 'tense and relax' muscle sequences or a visualisation sequence, for example 'going for a walk in the woods'.

Vocabulary

To quote Hap Palmer (2001) from his article featured in *Young Children*, 'Words that describe movement are a fundamental part of a child's vocabulary. To enhance a child's movement vocabulary is to enhance her overall vocabulary.' When we help children develop their language they have the means to describe and understand themselves and their place in the world about them. They will feel more self-confident and in control.

Try the following:

Body parts

Head, neck, shoulders, arms, fingers, thumbs, elbows, knees, legs, thighs, back, tummy, bottom, wrists, balls of feet, heels, ankles, toes, ears, nose, eyes, tongue

Actions

Walk, run, skip, hop, jump, step, stride, roll, balance, crouch, bounce, stretch, curl, twist, straighten, relax, weave in and out, bend, push, pull, travel, lie, sit, stand, tense, turn, rotate, lift, dart, relax, stay still, drop, swoop, rise, fall, lift, zig-zag

Actions with objects

Throw, catch, aim, drop, bounce, kick, dribble, hit

Directions in space

Right, left, different, same, opposite, together, facing, over, under, on, off, near, far, away, beside, going, coming, round, forwards, backwards, sideways, diagonally, on-the-spot, extend, near, far, middle, high, low

Shape

Long, thin, wide, narrow, huge, big, small, tiny

Speed

Fast, slow, slowly, quick, quickly, steady

When children are familiar with this basic list you can develop the vocabulary further and introduce the children's own suggestions. Try *quiver, wobble, scamper, float, glide, squidge* and so on.

Hello and welcome!

These activities are particularly suitable for a small group but can be adapted for one-to-one use, to set the scene and create a warm, friendly, positive experience. Choose the activities most suitable for the age range.

☐ Go round the group and say your name: *'Hello, I'm Ben'*.

☐ Go round the circle and give a thumbs up, saying, *'Hello, I'm Caroline'*.

☐ Go round the circle in turn and introduce the next child: *'I'm Amy, this is Fred…'*.

☐ Roll a ball across the circle saying name of recipient: *'This is for Anna'*.

☐ Pass a smile/hand-squeeze/frown/clap/hug/handshake one-to-one round the circle in turn. Pass it the other way.

☐ Pass a mascot or favourite toy round the circle. Say your own name as you pass a teddy or soft toy.

☐ Create silence in the room and ask, *'What can you hear?'*

☐ Send a whisper round the circle such as *'I'm happy because the sun is shining'*.

☐ Play *'I sit on the hill and I'd like Fred to come and sit next to me'*. Arrange an empty chair or space next to you and ask a child to come and sit beside you. This leaves an empty space for another child to choose someone to sit next to them.

☐ Pass a mirror at the bottom of a box round the group saying, *'In the box is a picture of the most important person in the whole room.'* Don't say anything until everyone has seen who the person is.

☐ Ask children to *'Stand up if you...*
- *have hair that is brown/black/ curly/long'*
- *are the youngest in your family'*
- *are wearing blue socks'*
- *feel happy'.*

☐ Go around the circle praising each child. For example, say, *'Emma is clever because she can . . . tie her laces/ride a bike/run fast/find her coat peg'.*

☐ Complete a 'round' such as *'I like going to...', 'My favourite food is...', 'I feel happy/sad when...', 'I like it when...'.*

☐ Share a 'round' by saying, *'I'm happy/sad/cross today because...'.*

☐ Ask children to *'Change places if you have brown hair/like eating sausages/are tall/have a sister'.*

☐ Pass the ring. Sit in a circle. Have a length of string that is long enough to reach round the circle, threaded through a ring and tied in a knot. One person starts by holding the ring that is then passed secretly from hand to hand, child to child, around the group. Children will need to be aware of each other and look for signs to guess where the ring is. They will need to be able to anticipate the ring coming to them and be sensitive to touch.

Stamina

If children do not walk far, run, swim or carry out physical activity for any length of time they will need the opportunity to develop stamina. Some children need to release energy before they can settle down to learn and some need physical action to diffuse and dissipate strong emotions such as fear and anger.

- [ ] Run around a circuit marked on the floor.

- [ ] Walk, hop, skip, jump around a circuit marked on the floor.

- [ ] Run, jump, skip or hop on the spot.

- [ ] Do star jumps, flinging arms and legs wide, then back together.

- [ ] Step on and off a step, bench or block, left foot then right foot.

- [ ] Walk quickly and stop.

- [ ] Run fast in any direction and stop.

- [ ] Take big strides around the room, on your own, with a partner.

- [ ] Bunny hops on the ground, or balancing arms on a bench, lifting two feet together in the air.

- [ ] Crouch down and jump up high, keep repeating for ten seconds.

- [ ] Crouch and jump a long way forward.

- [ ] Make two jumps away from a mat, two jumps forward, feet together.

- [ ] Throw a bean bag along the floor, run to collect it.

- [ ] Jump in and out of a hoop placed on the floor and repeat.

- [ ] Jump slowly then jump fast: forwards, backwards, sideways.

- [ ] Hop on left leg and then right leg on the spot. Try to hop forwards or backwards.

- [ ] Help a friend to hop by offering a hand to balance.

Large motor actions

This is the time to make large body movements, to feel the body in space, to co-ordinate parts into the whole.

- [ ] Cross-over: left hand to right knee, right hand to left knee, right hand to left foot raised behind, then left hand to right foot raised behind.

- [ ] Single-sided: lower right hand to meet right knee, then lower left hand to meet left knee.

- [ ] Play animals: walk, skip, jump or stand still when an animal name is called. For example, walk when you hear bear, stand still when you hear ostrich, jump when you hear rabbit, skip when you hear kangaroo.

- [ ] Lie on the floor and stretch out arms and legs to make a wide shape with your body, then pull in to make a thin shape.

- [ ] Roll along the floor stretched out, then roll the other way.

- [ ] Travel along the floor on tummy, back, bottom.

- [ ] Lie on the floor, move one body part at a time: lift head, hand, foot.

- [ ] Stand and make a wide body shape for partner to copy.

- [ ] Stand facing the wall, lean hands against the wall and push away.

- [ ] Travel round the room on 'all fours', forwards, backwards, sideways.

- [ ] Take strides as big as possible.

- [ ] On tummy: with hands by side, lift head off floor and hold for a count of three; with arms extended, lift and hold head and feet off floor.

- [ ] Jump and turn to face a new direction. Jump and turn 90 degrees. Repeat until back to the original position.

Mobility

This is about helping children to be supple and avoid problems with stiff joints and awkward movements generally. Some children are unable to isolate movements or develop fluid actions for sport where flexibility in the ankles, knees, hips, waist and shoulders is especially needed.

☐ Shoulders
- Lie on the floor, hands at side, sweep hands up and along the floor to meet above the head and clap.
- Lift arms over the head, down and sweep along the floor to sides.
- Stand, slowly rotate one shoulder, then the other, then together, rotate forwards then backwards.
- Stand, arms out at sides, palms facing up, then down and repeat.
- Stand, swing right arm, left arm, together, opposite. Encourage the knees to bend as arms drop and swoop.

☐ Spine
- Stand, arms above the head, stretch and bend forwards slowly.
- Lie on back, wiggle to feel whole spine against the floor, relax.

- On hands and knees, arch the back with head lowered, then hollow the back, raising head gently.

☐ Wrists
- Rotate wrists, left, right, together.
- Move wrists forwards, backwards, alternately.
- While sitting, place hands flat on floor, lift palms keeping fingertips in place.
- Place fingertips together, spread the hands, push together and feel the pressure on the wrists.

☐ Waist
- Stand, hands on hips and rotate upper body.

- Stand, hands on hips and swing upper body over to left side, right side.
- Stand, arms up above the head, gently flop down until fingertips brush the floor.

☐ Knees
  - Stand, gradually lower the body and up again.
  - Walking on the spot, lift knees high.
  - Face partner and copy their walking on the spot, keeping in pace.

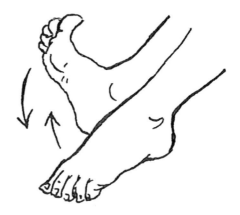

  - Crouch, place hands on the floor just in front of the feet and kick legs in the air.

☐ Hips
  - Lie on back, lift right leg in the air, swing across the body, lift and return.
  - Repeat with left leg.
  - Lie on side, body straight, lift top leg in air and down, roll over and repeat for the other leg.
  - Sit on the floor, legs straight, feet together, then open legs as wide as possible seeing how far apart the feet can go and return.
  - Sit cross-legged, hands on knees, gently push knees down towards floor.
  - Stand, hold onto the wall, swing right leg backwards and forwards, turn and repeat with the left leg.

☐ Ankles
  - Sit with legs straight out in front, push toes away, pull toes in.
  - Sit with legs straight out in front, let feet fall sideways outwards and come together.
  - Sit with legs straight out in front, rotate left ankle, right ankle, together.
  - Stand, rock from balls of feet to heels and back.
  - Walk on the spot, heel first.
  - Walk forward on toes, backwards on heels, eyes open, eyes closed.

Balance

A good sense of balance is important in all physical activities, requiring strength and tension. Children need good posture to sit on the floor in class during discussion times or at a desk without discomfort. Being 'in charge' of your body through balance brings feelings of security, confidence and well-being.

☐ Move anywhere in the room, stop and hold position.

☐ Stand on the balls of the feet, hands by side, fix eyes on a spot in front, count to three.

☐ Rock from toes to heels, straight body, bottom in, hands kept still by side.

☐ Stand on one foot for a count of three, stand on the other.

☐ Kneel up (not back on the heels), lift one knee off the ground.

☐ With weight on hands and knees, lift each arm forward in turn. Stretch each leg back in turn. Lift opposite arm and foot, lift same arm and foot.

☐ Stand and then slowly lower the body to a crouch.

☐ Kneel on left knee. Place right foot flat on the floor and place hands on right knee. Turn head to look over right shoulder, then left, without losing balance.

☐ Walk along a chalk line on the floor, head up. Forwards, sideways, backwards. Use a straight or curving line.

☐ Breathe in and lift hands in air. Breathe out and slowly bring arms down to the floor.

☐ Place weight on hands, bending body over, lift one leg, then the other. While bending over, keep hands still and make feet walk away from the body and then back again.

☐ Walk one foot in front of other, heel to toe.

☐ Stand on one leg and raise the other, balance with arms outstretched.

Body awareness

This allows us to understand different body parts and their relationship to each other in space.

☐ Posture
- Stand tall, head in midline, hold finger to tip of nose and draw head back a couple of centimetres
- Shoulders down, relax
- Hips level
- Feet hip-width apart
- Breathe slowly in and out.

☐ Back
- Lie on the floor, make all of the back touch the floor, wriggle and rub back and shoulders on the floor
- Stand against a wall and feel all of back on the wall.

☐ Elbows
- Touch elbows, bend and straighten, right, left, together, eyes open, eyes closed
- Elbow high, low, rotate, slowly, quickly, trace pattern in the air
- Elbows touching floor, left, right, together
- Elbows touch knee, right to left, right to right, left to right, left to left.

☐ Knees
- Sit and pat knees with hands then with elbows
- Sit and bend knees up to the chin, push knees down with hands until legs are straight
- Stand, bend one knee up as far as possible
- Sit on the floor, feet touch sole to sole, knees fall out sideways and then bring knees back in together.

☐ Stand with right arm stretched out, index finger pointing, twist to the right from the waist, with your eyes following the finger to see how far round you can see. Now fix your eyes on a spot on the wall. Have another go and try to see further round this time. Repeat with your left hand, twisting to the left.

☐ Child closes eyes and uses a ball or bean bag to touch body parts as called out by the adult, as fast as possible.

☐ Travel round the room with certain body parts leading – hands, feet, bottom, knees, head. Child copies actions of a partner.

☐ Flex and stretch body parts in sequence standing or sitting: nod head, rotate shoulder, stretch and curl hand, tighten tummy, clench bottom, bend legs then make them stiff and straight, rotate ankles, squidge and wiggle toes.

Spatial awareness

Knowledge and awareness of our own body in space, judging distances and using appropriate interpersonal space can bring personal confidence and be important in building good relationships with others.

- ☐ Stand, bend over, touch toes, letting knees bend, uncurl slowly from base of spine to standing, head uncurls last of all.

- ☐ On mat, make as small a shape as possible, as large a shape as possible.

- ☐ Stand, legs apart, arms wide, close up slowly.

- ☐ Stand next to a partner, move apart until you can just touch fingertips or feet.

- ☐ Weave around bean bags/skittles spaced along the floor in circles or lines.

- ☐ Run around on 'all fours'.

- ☐ Run/walk around an imaginary circle, snake pattern, zig-zag, eyes open, eyes closed.

- ☐ Child puts hand on shoulder of partner or adult and is 'led' around the room, eyes open, eyes closed.

- ☐ Crawl through hoop without touching the sides.

- ☐ Walk by sliding feet, feet staying in contact with the floor at all times.

- ☐ Reach high with both hands, then touch the floor.

- ☐ Eyes closed, draw a large circle in the air, right hand, left hand, together.

- ☐ Walk or jump right, left, forwards, backwards, diagonally, eyes open, eyes closed.

- ☐ Stand opposite a partner and copy their movements.

- ☐ Stand opposite a partner and touch fingertips. One partner 'leads' fingers of the other in making large circles in the air.

Dexterity

Children may need help in being able to grasp and release small objects. Often both hands will not work together. There is not enough strength or hands may be too floppy to grasp and hold a ball or other small object such as a pencil. Eye–hand co-ordination may be weak.

☐ Awareness of fingers
- Spread your fingers
- Stretch and curl
- Count fingers
- Move fingers independently
- Match fingers of both hands together, palm to palm
- Match fingers with a partner, touch one by one.

☐ Wrists
- Rotate right wrist, one way then the other
- Rotate left wrist
- Rotate both together
- Rotate quickly as if whisking a cake
- Rotate slowly watching all the movements of the bones
- Rotate close to the body and as far away as possible.

☐ Thumbs
- Thumb up, thumb down, left hand, right hand, together
- Opposite thumbs up or down
- Touch thumb to fingers one at a time using left hand, right hand, then together.

☐ Using fingers
- Sit on the mat, use fingertips to roll a large ball round your mat
- Use left hand, right hand, together
- Walk hands along the floor – fast like a spider, then slowly like a caterpillar.

☐ Throwing
- Throw a bean bag onto a mat
- Throw a bean bag onto a cross on a mat
- Throw from one metre, two metres
- Throw to a partner's mat
- Throw a small ball into a box, large ball into a box.

☐ Aiming
- Throw a bean bag onto a cross on the floor, into a box, through a hoop, over a mat
- Roll a ball towards a skittle
- Sit on the floor, push a ball towards a partner.

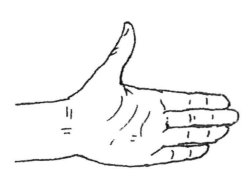
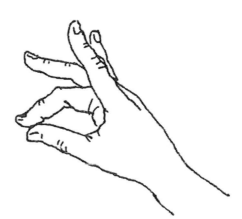

☐ Catching
  - Sit with legs wide, catch a large ball rolled along the ground
  - Sit and catch a large ball thrown to you
  - Stand and catch a large ball, then a small ball
  - Catch a bean bag thrown to you
  - Catch with one hand, then the other
  - Bounce and catch a ball.

☐ Kicking
  - Kick a large ball towards a skittle
  - Kick a small ball
  - Kick between two skittles
  - Kick a ball to a partner.

☐ Dribbling
  - Push a ball with one foot
  - Push/kick a ball keeping it close to your foot
  - Dribble a ball in and out of a row of skittles.

Fine motor skills

Young children enjoy playing and experimenting with different objects and materials. These activities demand concentration and a degree of precision, and so will help to develop their fine motor skills co-ordination.

☐ Pick up small items using chopsticks or tongs.

☐ Cut with scissors. Cut straight lines, curved lines, geometric shapes such as squares, triangles or rectangles, fringes. Cut out shapes following dots or faint lines. Cut into folded paper to make paper mats. Cut with pinking shears.

☐ Stencils and templates. Draw round templates made of plastic, wood or card, or round small objects such as boxes or cups. Also draw within template frames. Draw round natural objects such as feathers, stones, leaves. Draw round your feet or hands. Draw round a partner's body.

☐ Lacing. Use a card punched with holes and thread with a shoe lace or string.

☐ Learn to plait using three strands of ribbon or wool.

☐ Thread beads with gradually smaller shapes and finer holes. Use cotton reels or macaroni for a change.

☐ Post shapes or coins into holes or slots at speed. Try placing shapes in a shape-sorter or puzzle tray against the clock.

☐ Colour using different pens, pencils or chalks. Try using triangular pencils or pencil grips. Try colouring big shapes on the floor or wall.

☐ Paper folding or origami. Simple paper folding is useful for hand–eye co-ordination.

☐ Follow dot-to-dot patterns or pictures using a finger or pencil.

☐ Mazes with increasing complexity. Use your finger to follow around lines in the flooring, on equipment or wallpaper.

☐ Circles. Draw circles on paper or large circles on a chalk board. Try left hand, right hand and both hands, clockwise and counter-clockwise. Draw circles in the air. Copy or mirror a friend.

☐ Jacks/pick up sticks. Play jacks to develop hand–eye co-ordination, rhythmical movements, fine finger and hand movements. See how many small stones or marbles you can pick up in one hand.

- [ ] Clothes pegs. Clip clothes pegs on a line or around the rim of a box. Children can be timed – 'How many pegs in a minute?' or 'How quickly you can place ten pegs?'

- [ ] Place pegs in a peg-board.

- [ ] Fastenings: zips, buttons, catches, removing and replacing lids, screwing and unscrewing lids.

- [ ] Hammering nails into soft wood.

- [ ] Clay-work, play dough, plasticene. Try rolling material into sausage shapes, pat flat, model into other shapes.

- [ ] Utilise Lego®, Meccano® and other construction toys and jigsaws.

- [ ] Water play using pouring and carrying activities. Use smaller amounts and finer measurements to make the task more difficult.

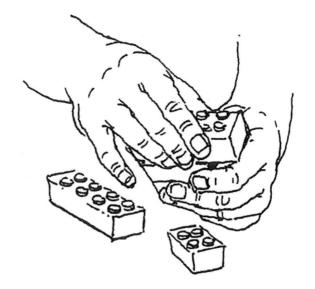

Rhythm and sequence

Activities in this section are designed to develop fluidity of movement and attention to rhythm and repetition, and to let children enjoy mastery of sequences of actions. They can create their own actions to teach others or copy their peers.

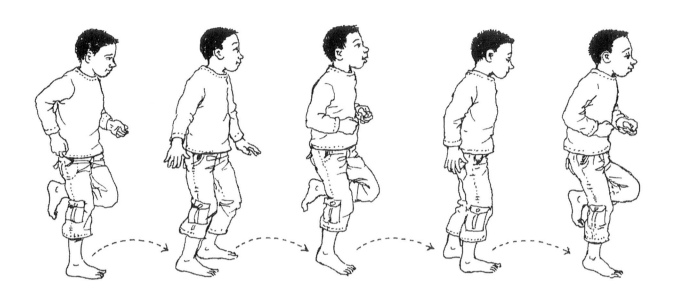

- Clap with steady beat, slowly, quickly. Make a rhythm such as clap clap stop clap clap stop. Child copies a partner.

- Jump forward two steps, backwards two steps, repeat.

- Step-hop-step-hop sequence.

- Left foot forward, feet together, right foot forward, feet together.

- March on the spot and count 1, 2, 1, 2 or left, right, left, right.

- Marching round the room, swing arms to the rhythm of a tambourine or claves. Walk quickly, walk slowly, following a beat.

- Drop and catch a ball rhythmically.

- Bounce a ball on the floor, left hand, right hand, alternate hands.

- Start at one end of the room and work out a sequence such as jump, hop, step and repeat until you reach the other end of the room.

- Sit on the floor, legs wide apart, opposite partner and roll ball backwards and forwards.

- Stand or sit on the floor and make up sequence such as clap, pat knees, stamp feet.

- Pass a bean bag from left hand to right hand and back, to a rhythmic count or metronome. Then try in front of the body and behind the back.

- Slide left foot sideways and then right foot to meet it, repeat.

Relaxation

The aim of this section is to teach children how to relax, how to soothe themselves and calm down. Think about the environmental factors to help relaxation such as low lighting, warmth, quiet, soft cushions, calm music.

- [ ] Shake the body all over until every part has moved. Name the body parts in turn to be shaken and then encourage all over shaking.

- [ ] Wriggle toes, relax feet, make feet feel heavy, then soft and floppy, make legs feel tired, heavy, full of lead.

- [ ] Lie on floor, slowly spread out to make a wide shape, slowly curl up. Encourage smooth flowing actions by counting.

- [ ] Curl your toes, tense up and then let go. Repeat several times to a count of five.

- [ ] Squeeze hands and make a fist, let go and make hands feel floppy.

- [ ] The plant or tree:
  Ask children to stand and gradually feel themselves rooted to the spot. Suggest that each part of the body becomes heavy in turn so that they feel leaden, saggy and well grounded.

- [ ] Stand, lift arms, make five big circles one way, then the other way, rotating from the shoulders. Start using quick rotations, then gradually slow down and stop.

- [ ] Stretch neck, slowly let head fall until chin falls onto chest.

- [ ] Breathe in deeply through the nose to a count of four and breathe out through the mouth to a count of four. Count your breaths and say the number as you breathe out to avoid distractions.

- [ ] Guided visualisation:
  - Sit or lie on the floor.
  - Close your eyes.
  - Think of a favourite place where you feel safe, happy and peaceful.
  - Gradually describe what you might see, hear, smell, taste, touch.
  - For example, *'The sun is shining, the sky is a deep blue, you are sitting with a friend, you are sitting on the sand by the sea and can hear the waves gently coming in and out, washing over the sea shore. You can hear the cry of a sea gull, taste the salt in the air and feel the warm sun on your face... Gradually come back to the world, open your eyes and when you feel ready, roll onto your side and slowly sit up.'*

  - You can take children on an imaginary walk through the woods or park, or through their own home. Choose things that are within their experience or use a picture to set the scene.

- [ ] Gently massage own feet, starting toe by toe and then make larger smoothing strokes over the soles.

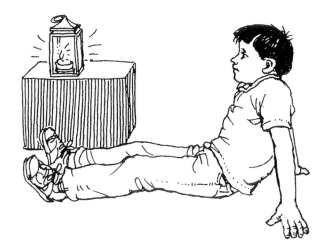

☐ Light a candle and sit quietly looking at the flame. Try using an aromatic candle and adding music. Follow the health and safety advice for your own situation and only use a flame where it is safe and legal to do so. An electric flickering flame bulb could be as effective.

☐ Sit quietly and listen to music – some classical music or 'healing' music.

☐ Scrunch and let go:
   - Sit or lie on the floor, eyes open or closed.
   - Ask children to tense a group of muscles, hold that state of tension for a few seconds and then relax.
   - For example, *'Clench your fist into a ball, hold for three seconds and then relax. Now scrunch all the parts of your face into a funny shape, hold and let go. Now tense the muscles in your bottom, hold and relax.'*

☐ Progressive muscle relaxation:
   - Sit or lie comfortably on the floor.
   - Close your eyes.
   - Ask children to relax the muscles of their body progressively as you guide them through.
   - For example, *'Think about your face and make your eyes relax, make your mouth relax and your nose relax. Now think of your neck muscles and let go of any tension there. Let your shoulders sink down, then your arms and hands. Make your tummy relax and your back and bottom. Now think about your legs and make them feel heavy. Lastly, let your feet relax.'*
   - You may like to test the state of relaxation by gently lifting a child's arm or leg to see if it will flop down in a relaxed way.

☐ The rainforest:
   - Sitting in a circle, ask children to tap, clap, pat and then stamp to make the sound of a rainstorm in the forest.
   - Start by clapping using one finger tapping the palm of the other hand; one by one, children follow this action until everyone in the group is tapping.
   - Then use two fingers to tap the other hand and 'pass' this round the circle.
   - Next, increase the sound of the 'rain' by clapping palm to palm, followed by patting knees and then stamping feet.
      - When everyone has reached this stage 'undo' the sequence (stamping – patting – clapping – tapping two fingers, one finger) until the noise of the 'rain' dies away.

Session 1

Hello and welcome

Sitting in a circle

☐ Roll a ball across the circle saying name of recipient
   - I can make contact with others

☐ Go around the circle and give a thumbs up saying, *'Hello, I'm Caroline'*
   - I can greet other people

☐ Share a 'round' in the circle saying, *'I'm feeling happy, sad or cross today'*
   - I can say how I'm feeling

☐ Pass the hand squeeze round the circle
   - I belong in this group

Getting going

Use the space in the hall or room

☐ Run around a circuit marked on the floor
   - I can keep going

☐ Walk, hop, skip, jump around a circuit marked on the floor
   - I can follow a track

☐ March on the spot and count 1, 2, 1, 2 or left, right, left, right

☐ Marching around the room, swing arms to the rhythm of a tambourine or claves

☐ Walk quickly, walk slowly, following a beat
   - I can co-ordinate my movements

Stop and pause

Use a confined space

☐ Stand on the balls of the feet, hands by side, fix eyes on a spot in front, count to three
   - I can balance

☐ Rock from toes to heels, straight body, bottom in, hands kept still by side

☐ Elbows
   - Touch elbows, bend and straighten, right, left, together, eyes open, eyes closed
   - Elbow high, low, rotate, slowly, quickly, trace a pattern in the air
   - Elbows touching floor, left, right, together
   - Elbows touch knees, right to left, right to right, left to right, left to left
     - I can move parts of my body

☐ Close eyes and use a ball or bean bag to touch body parts as called by the adult, as fast as possible

☐ Stand opposite a partner and copy their movements
   - I can notice other people

☐ Stand opposite a partner and touch fingertips. One partner 'leads' fingers of the other by making large circles in the air
   - I can mirror other people

Peace at last

Use the space but stay close together

- ☐ Shake your body all over until every part has moved. Name body parts in turn to be shaken and then encourage all over shaking
  - I am aware of every part of my body

- ☐ Breathe in deeply through the nose to a count of four and breathe out through the mouth to a count of four. Count your breaths and say the number as you breathe out to avoid distractions
  - I know how to relax

- ☐ Light a candle and sit quietly looking at the flame
  - I can sit quietly

Session 1 - Explanations

Hello and welcome

Sitting in a circle

☐ Roll a ball across the circle saying the name of the recipient
  - Sit in a circle, legs out straight and open. Take a large ball and roll it across to someone in the group. You may like to say, *'This is for Kathy'* as you roll the ball. They will then roll the ball to someone new, saying that child's name as they do so.

☐ Go around the circle and give a thumbs up saying, *'Hello, I'm Caroline'*
  - Still sitting in the circle, start the 'Hellos' by giving good eye contact to one child in the group. The child gives the thumbs up sign saying, *'Hello, I'm Jack'*. Take it in turns until everyone has introduced themselves.

☐ Share a 'round' in the circle saying, *'I'm feeling happy, sad or cross today'*
  - Begin to introduce varied vocabulary to express more subtle emotions such as *disappointed, worried, afraid*. This is a good way to check how everyone is feeling and to off-load any strong emotions that could interfere with the session.

☐ Pass the hand squeeze round the circle
  - As you sit in the circle, hold hands round the group. Start a squeeze with the child on your right. They then squeeze the hand of the child on their right.

Try this with eyes closed and feel the squeeze coming. Try starting another hand squeeze going the other way round the circle.

Getting going

Use the space in the hall or room

☐ Run around a circuit marked on the floor
  - Ask children to run around a track or line marked on the floor. Use chalk or tape to mark out the pathway.

☐ Walk, hop, skip, jump around a circuit marked on the floor
  - Encourage careful and accurate movements. Support children who find it hard to hop or skip. These movements could be taught separately at other times such as PE or break times.

☐ March on the spot and count 1, 2, 1, 2 or left, right, left, right
  - Use a tambourine, claves or metronome to mark the beat.

☐ Marching around the room, swing arms to the rhythm of a tambourine or claves.

☐ Walk quickly, walk slowly, following a beat
  - Encourage children to sense the change in pace and make a marked difference.

Stop and pause

Use a confined space

- ☐ Stand on the balls of the feet, hands by side, fix eyes on a spot in front, count to three
  - Children may need a supporting hand or somewhere to lean against to balance on the balls of their feet. Encourage children to count for themselves to set their own pace. Lengthen the time to a count of five if possible.

- ☐ Rock from toes to heels, straight body, bottom in, hands kept still by side
  - Ask children to feel the tension in their feet as they rock. Offer a hand to help them keep their balance.

- ☐ Elbows
  - Touch elbows, bend and straighten, right, left, together, eyes open, eyes closed
  - Elbow high, low, rotate, slowly, quickly, trace a pattern in the air
  - Elbows touching floor, left, right, together
  - Elbows touch knees, right to left, right to right, left to right, left to left.

- ☐ Close eyes and use a ball or bean bag to touch body parts as called by the adult, as fast as possible
  - Children can call out body parts in turn or one child leads the group.

- ☐ Stand opposite a partner and copy their movements
  - You may need to suggest an action to give some ideas, such as brushing your hair, sweeping the floor, painting a wall.

- ☐ Stand opposite a partner and touch fingertips. One partner 'leads' fingers of the other by making large circles in the air
  - To start with this may need a third party to guide the fingers in making circles.

Peace at last

Use the space but stay close together

- ☐ Shake body all over until every part has moved
  - Ask children to shake each part of their body in turn as you name it – then shake the whole body. Be still and notice any sensations or after shocks.

- ☐ Breathe in deeply through the nose to the count of four and breathe out through the mouth to a count of four
  - Encourage children to keep their shoulders down with relaxed chest and tummy. Start with a count of two and see if they can extend their breath control to counts of five or six.

- ☐ Light a candle and sit quietly looking at the flame
  - Ask the children to sit looking at the flame and to feel quiet and calm inside. The flame provides a focus of interest – better than having the children simply look at each other. An aromatic candle can provide a smell to stimulate the senses and calm the body. You may wish to add music at this point.

Session 2

Hello and welcome

Sitting in a circle

☐ Go round the circle in turn and introduce the next child, *'I'm Amy, this is Fred...'*
 - I know the people in my group

☐ Pass a smile, then a frown one-to-one round the circle in turn. Pass it the other way
 - I know how to make contact with others

☐ Pass a mascot or favourite toy round the circle
 - I can share something special with others

☐ Ask children to change places: *'If you have brown hair/like eating sausages/are tall/have a sister'*
 - I can listen to instructions

☐ Complete a 'round': *'My favourite food is...'*
 - I can express my likes

Getting going

Use the space in the hall or room

☐ Run, jump, skip or hop on the spot
 - I can stay in one place

☐ Star jumps, flinging arms and legs wide, then back together
 - I can co-ordinate my movements

☐ Step on and off a step, bench or block, left foot then right foot

☐ Step–hop–step–hop sequence

☐ Start at one end of the room and work out a sequence such as jump, hop, step and repeat
 - I can remember a sequence

Stop and pause

Using a more confined space

☐ Stand on one foot for a count of three, stand on the other
 - I can balance

☐ Stand and then slowly lower body to a crouch
 - I can be very controlled

☐ Stand with right arm stretched out, index finger pointing, twist to the right from the waist, with your eyes following the finger to see how far you can see round. Now fix your eyes on a spot on the wall. Have another go and try to see further round this time. Repeat with your left hand, twisting to the left
 - I am aware of my limits

☐ Crawl through a hoop without touching the sides
 - I am aware of my body space

☐ Walk by sliding feet, feet staying in contact with the floor at all times

☐ Reach high with both hands, then touch the floor
 - I can spread out

☐ Eyes closed, draw a large circle in the air, right hand, left hand, together
 - I am aware of my body in space

Peace at last

Use the space but stay close together

☐ Wriggle toes, relax feet, make feet feel heavy, then soft and floppy, make legs feel tired, heavy, full of lead
 - I can slow down

☐ Guided visualisation
 - I can calm myself

Session 2 - Explanations

Hello and welcome

Sitting in a circle

- ☐ Go round the circle in turn and introduce the next child: *'I'm Amy, this is Fred...'*
  - Children should now be feeling confident with each other and happy to be part of the group. This activity is about belonging and welcoming others.

- ☐ Pass a smile, then a frown one-to-one round the circle in turn. Pass it the other way
  - This activity is about noticing facial expressions and how it feels to give and receive different messages.

- ☐ Pass a mascot or favourite toy round the circle
  - Children may like to bring a favourite toy to show and share. This is about getting to know what other children find precious and respecting that.

- ☐ Ask children to change places *'If you have brown hair/like eating sausages/are tall/have a sister'*
  - This activity is about noticing our own attributes and comparing with others.

- ☐ Complete a 'round': *'My favourite food is...'*
  - This should be an easy round for children to take part in. However, as with any round, if children are shy and lack confidence they should be allowed to pass.

Getting going

Using the whole space of the hall or room

- ☐ Run, jump, skip or hop on the spot
  - Children may need help to develop hopping and skipping. Place a hoop on the floor and see if children can keep within this limit.

- ☐ Star jumps, flinging arms and legs wide, then back together
  - Children may need to learn this in parts, making arm movements separately from leg movements, then putting the actions together.

- ☐ Step on and off a step, bench or block, left foot then right foot
  - If there is no bench available just step forward and backwards.

- ☐ Step–hop–step–hop sequence
  - Guide children as to which foot to use to make the step, then the hop.

- ☐ Start at one end of the room and work out a sequence such as jump, hop, step and repeat
  - Start with just two actions to repeat and then add another.

Stop and pause

Using a more confined space

- ☐ Stand on one foot for a count of three, then stand on the other
  - Children may like to help each other to balance and to count for each other

- ☐ Stand and then slowly lower body to a crouch
  - This could be done individually or in pairs or as a circle activity, holding hands.

- ☐ Stand with right arm stretched out, index finger pointing, twist to the right from the waist, with your eyes following the finger to see how far you can see round. Now fix your eyes on a spot on the wall. Have another go and try to see further round this time. Repeat with your left hand, twisting to the left
  - This is an interesting activity to see how gently moving the body further each time can extend the range of vision.

- ☐ Crawl through a hoop without touching the sides
  - Encourage children to help each other by holding the hoop and guiding their friends.

- ☐ Walk by sliding feet, feet staying in contact with the floor at all times
  - If feet are sticky use talcum powder and look at the slide marks.

- ☐ Reach high with both hands, then touch the floor
  - A variation of the earlier activity that involves stretching and lowering.

- ☐ Eyes closed, draw a large circle in the air, right hand, left hand, together
  - Again, ask children to look at each other and guide their friends to make good circles.

Peace at last

Use the space but stay close together

- ☐ Wriggle toes, relax feet, make feet feel heavy, then soft and floppy, make legs feel tired, heavy, full of lead
  - There is a lot of vocabulary here and children may need demonstrations to understand what is being asked and how it feels. The activity is a good beginning to a relaxation sequence.

- ☐ Guided visualisation:
  - Sit or lie on the floor.
  - Close your eyes.
  - Think of a favourite place where you feel safe, happy and peaceful.
  - Gradually describe what you might see, hear, smell, taste, touch.
  - For example, *'The sun is shining, the sky is a deep blue, you are sitting with a friend, you are sitting on the sand by the sea and can hear the waves gently coming in and out, washing over the sea shore. You can hear the cry of a sea gull, taste the salt in the air and feel the warm sun on your face... Gradually come back to the world, open your eyes and when you feel ready, roll onto your side and slowly sit up.'*
  - You can take children on an imaginary walk through the woods or park, or through their own home. Choose things that are within their experience or use a picture to set the scene.

Session 3

Hello and welcome

Sitting in a circle

☐ Go round the group and say your name: *'Hello, I'm Ben'*
- - I know how to introduce myself

☐ Create silence in the room and ask children *'What can you hear?'*
- - I know how to listen carefully

☐ Send a whisper around the circle such as *'I'm happy because the sun is shining'*
- - I can take turns

Getting going

Using the whole space of the hall or room

☐ Take big strides around the room, on your own, with a partner
- - I can make big movements

☐ Crouch down and jump up high, keep repeating for ten seconds
- - I can make springing movements

☐ Crouch and jump a long way forward
- - I can spring into action

☐ Roll along the floor stretched out, roll the other way
- - I can stretch out

☐ Travel along the floor on your tummy, back, bottom
- - I can move other parts of my body

☐ Travel around the room on 'all fours', forwards, backwards, sideways
- - I can find other ways to travel, not just walking

Stop and pause

Using a more confined space

☐ Move anywhere in the room, stop and hold position
- - I know how to move and stop

☐ Kneel up (not back on heels), lift one knee off the ground
- - I can control different parts of my body

☐ Put your weight on your hands and knees, lift each arm forward in turn, stretch each leg back in turn. Lift opposite arm and foot, lift same arm and foot
- - I am aware of the weight of my body

☐ Kneel on your left knee. Place right foot flat on the floor and place hands on your right knee. Turn head to look over right shoulder, then left, without losing balance
- - I can balance

☐ Sit on the floor, legs wide apart, opposite partner and roll ball backwards and forwards
- - I can anticipate and respond to others

☐ Sit on the floor and make up a sequence such as clap, pat knees, stamp feet
- - I can remember a sequence

☐ On the mat, make as small a shape as possible, as large a shape as possible
- - I am aware of my size

☐ Stand, legs apart, arms wide, close up slowly
  - I can change shape

☐ Stand next to a partner, move further apart until you can just touch fingertips or feet
  - I am aware of social space

Peace at last

Use the space but stay close together

☐ Curl your toes, tense up and then let go. Repeat several times to a count of five
  - I know about being tense or relaxed

☐ Squeeze hands and make a fist, let go and make hands feel floppy
  - I can be strong and gentle

☐ Gently massage your own feet, starting toe by toe and then make larger smoothing strokes over the soles
  - I can soothe myself

Session 3 - Explanations

Hello and welcome

Sitting in a circle

☐ Go round the group and say your name: *'Hello, I'm Ben'*
  - Another 'getting to know you game', encouraging the confidence to introduce yourself and greet others appropriately.

☐ Create silence in the room and ask the children *'What can you hear?'*
  - Listen to noises outside the room such as traffic, children playing, bird song, rain. This activity encourages listening skills – a good way to start a session where children need to listen to instructions carefully. As an alternative you may like to ask children to point in the direction of sounds rather than naming what they can hear. Vary the activity by asking children to close their eyes and point towards the sound as you move around the group shaking a tambourine.

☐ Send a whisper around the circle such as *'I'm happy because the sun is shining'*
  - Another activity to encourage concentration and listening skills.

Getting going

Using the whole space of the hall or room

☐ Take big strides around the room, on your own, with a partner.

☐ Crouch down and jump up high, keep repeating for ten seconds
  - An activity to encourage sudden springing movements.

☐ Crouch and jump a long way forward.

☐ Roll along the floor stretched out, roll the other way
  - Encourage children to stretch first and hold this position before they roll, then to keep a stretched form.

☐ Travel along the floor on your tummy, back, bottom
  - A good opportunity to be aware of parts of the body we do not usually use for moving.

☐ Travel around the room on 'all fours', forwards, backwards, sideways
  - Again, ask children to make the shape first and then move. Make sure they are aware of others around them and do not collide.

Stop and pause

Using a more confined space

☐ Move anywhere in the room, stop and hold position.

☐ Kneel up (not back on heels), lift one knee off the ground.

☐ Put your weight on your hands and knees, lift each arm forward in turn, stretch each leg back in turn. Lift opposite arm and foot, lift same arm and foot
  - Take time to look at the body shapes produced. See if children can hold the stretched shape for a couple of seconds.

☐ Kneel on your left knee. Place right foot flat on the floor and place hands on your right knee. Turn head to look

over right shoulder, then left, without losing balance
- Ask children to pick out a spot on the wall to look at. See if next time they can see even further round.

☐ Sit on the floor, legs wide apart, opposite partner and roll ball backwards and forwards
- As a variation, change the size or weight of the ball.

☐ Sit on the floor and make up a sequence such as clap, pat knees, stamp feet
- Ask the children to suggest their own sequence for others to copy.

☐ On the mat, make as small a shape as possible, as large a shape as possible
- If there is time, ask children to work in pairs where one makes a large shape around the other's small shape.

☐ Stand, legs apart, arms wide, close up slowly.

☐ Stand next to a partner, move further apart until you can just touch fingertips or feet
- Use this to explain intimate, social or public space and illustrate the difference.

Peace at last

Use the space but stay close together

☐ Curl your toes, tense up and then let go. Repeat several times to a count of five
- Focus on one part of the body. Use counting to reduce distractions and set the pace for the movement. As with the next activity, children will learn tension and relaxation and can begin to create a self-help routine.

☐ Squeeze hands and make a fist, let go and make hands feel floppy
- Look at what others are doing and compare the size and shape of the fist.

☐ Gently massage your own feet, starting toe by toe and then make larger smoothing strokes over the tops and soles
- Encourage smooth, gentle actions, explore each part of the toes, top, sole, ankle and heel. This gentle massage can provide a focus for relaxation and, again, a self-help calming and soothing routine.

Session 4

Hello and welcome

Sitting in a circle

☐ Roll a ball across the circle saying the name of the recipient: *'This is for Anna'*
  - I can greet other people

☐ Play *'I sit on the hill and I'd like Fred to come and sit next to me'*
  - I can welcome others

☐ Pass a clap around the circle
  - I can lead a group or follow others

Getting going

Using the whole space of the hall or room

☐ Walk quickly and stop
  - I can manage to stop and start

☐ Run fast in any direction and stop

☐ Weave around bean bags or skittles spaced along the floor in a circle or line
  - I can be careful and not knock into things

☐ Run around on 'all fours'
  - I can move in different ways

☐ Run or walk around an imaginary circle, snake pattern, zig-zag, eyes open, eyes closed
  - I am aware of how my body moves

Stop and pause

Using a more confined space

☐ Walk one foot in front of the other, heel to toe
  - I can make small, careful movements

☐ Stand on one leg and raise the other, balance with arms outstretched

☐ Wrists
  - Rotate wrists, left, right, together
  - Move wrists forwards, backwards, alternately
  - Place hands flat on the floor, lift palms keeping fingertips in place
  - Place fingertips together, spread the hands, push together and feel the pressure on the wrists
    - I can develop fluid movement and suppleness

☐ Waist
  - Stand, hands on hips and rotate upper body
  - Stand, hands on hips, swing upper body over to the left side, the right side
  - Stand, arms up above the head, gently flop down until fingertips brush the floor

☐ Child puts hand on shoulder of partner or adult and is 'led' around the room, eyes open, eyes closed
  - I know how to trust others

☐ Eyes closed, draw a large circle in the air, right hand, left hand, together
  - I can move my body by feeling the way

Peace at last

Use the space but stay close together

☐ Lie on the floor, slowly spread out to make a wide shape, slowly curl up
  - I can feel how big my body can be and how small

☐ The plant or tree
  - I feel grounded

☐ The rainforest
  - I can take my part in a group activity

Session 4 - Explanations

Hello and welcome

Sitting in a circle

☐ Roll a ball across the circle saying the name of the recipient: *'This is for Anna'*
  - This is a game to encourage a sense of belonging and being part of the group. It feels good to be welcomed by name.

☐ Play *'I sit on the hill and I'd like Fred to come and sit next to me'*
  - Arrange an empty chair or space next to you and ask a child to come and sit beside you. This leaves an empty space for another child to choose someone to sit next to them. Encourage the children to choose a different person each time and make sure all the children are chosen.

☐ Pass a clap around the circle
  - There can be lots of variation here using a single clap or sequence for the next child to copy in turn. As children become more confident they can make up their own special way of clapping for others to copy and start leading the group.

Getting going

Using the whole space of the hall or room

☐ Walk quickly and stop
  - Ask children to stop when they feel like it or use a signal for everyone to stop together.

☐ Run fast in any direction and stop
  - Make sure children are aware of others and do not collide. It may be necessary to ask children to go one at a time.

☐ Weave around bean bags or skittles spaced along the floor in a circle or line
  - Children may do this quickly or slowly, walking or travelling on other parts of the body.

☐ Run around on 'all fours'.

☐ Run or walk around an imaginary circle, snake pattern, zig-zag, eyes open, eyes closed
  - Start by asking children to walk carefully and gradually allow faster movements. Again, children may need to go one at a time to start with.

Stop and pause

Using a more confined space

☐ Walk one foot in front of the other, heel to toe
  - This activity and the next require balance and control. Children could give a helping hand to each other.

☐ Stand on one leg and raise the other, balance with arms outstretched.

☐ Wrists
  - Rotate wrists, left, right, together Move wrists forwards, backwards, alternately
  - Place hands flat on the floor, lift palms keeping fingertips in place
  - Place fingertips together, spread the hands, push together and feel the pressure on the wrists
  - This activity and the next explore parts of the body that bend, twist and rotate. See how smooth the actions can be and practise to develop suppleness.

- [ ] Waist
    - Stand, hands on hips, and rotate upper body
    - Stand, hands on hips, swing upper body over to the left side, the right side
    - Stand, arms up above the head, gently flop down until fingertips brush the floor

- [ ] Child puts hand on shoulder of partner or adult and is 'led' around the room, eyes open, eyes closed
    - With eyes closed, this is an activity that develops trust between children or adults and children.

- [ ] Eyes closed, draw a large circle in the air, right hand, left hand, together
    - Ask children to watch each other to check the circles or gently guide their movements.

Peace at last

Use the space but stay close together

- [ ] Lie on the floor, slowly spread out to make a wide shape, slowly curl up
    - Children may like to watch each other. Again, count slowly to encourage fluid actions.

- [ ] The plant or tree
    - Ask children to stand and gradually feel themselves rooted to the spot. Suggest that each part of the body becomes heavy in turn so that they feel leaden, saggy and well grounded. Ask children to notice how they feel and suggest words to describe their state.

- [ ] The rainforest
    - Sitting in a circle, ask children to tap, clap, pat and stamp to make the sound of a rainstorm in the forest. Start by clapping using one finger tapping the palm of the other hand. One by one, children follow this action until everyone in the group is tapping. Then use two fingers to tap the other hand and 'pass' this round the circle. Increase the sound by clapping palm to palm, followed by patting knees and then stamping feet. When everyone has reached this stage 'undo' the sequence (stamping – patting – clapping – tapping) until the noise of the 'rain' dies away.

Session 5

Hello and welcome

Sitting in a circle

- [ ] Say your own name as you pass a teddy or soft toy
  - I can share something special

- [ ] Ask children to *'Stand up if you… have hair that is brown/black/curly/ long, are the youngest in your family, are wearing blue socks, feel happy'*
  - I know special things about me

- [ ] Pass a frown around the circle. Then pass it the other way. Follow the frown by a smile. Then ask children to choose or mirror what is passed on by the previous child
  - I can read expressions

Getting going

Using the whole space of the hall or room

- [ ] Jump in and out of a hoop placed on the floor and repeat
  - I'm getting better at jumping

- [ ] Jump slowly, then jump fast: forwards, backwards, sideways

- [ ] Cross-over: left hand to right knee, right hand to left knee, right hand to left foot raised behind, then left hand to right foot raised behind
  - I can cross the mid-line

- [ ] Single-sided: lower your right hand to meet your right knee, then lower your left hand to meet your left knee
  - I can keep both sides separate

Stop and pause

Using a more confined space

- [ ] Breathe in and lift hands in the air. Breathe out and slowly bring arms down to the floor
  - I can move slowly and purposefully

- [ ] Awareness of fingers
  - spread your fingers
  - stretch and curl
  - count fingers
  - move fingers independently
  - match fingers together, palm to palm
  - match fingers with a partner's touch one by one
    - I am aware of parts of my body

- [ ] Ankles
  - sit with legs straight out in front, push toes away, pull toes in
  - sit with legs straight out in front, let feet fall sideways outwards and come together
  - sit with legs straight out in front, rotate left ankle, right ankle, together
  - stand, rock from balls of feet to heels and back
  - walk on the spot, heel first
  - walk forward on toes, backwards on heels, eyes open, eyes closed

- [ ] Thumbs
  - thumb up, thumb down, left hand, right hand, together
  - opposite thumbs up or down
  - touch thumb to fingers one at a time using left hand, right hand, then together

☐ Using fingers
  - sit on the mat, use fingertips to roll a large ball round your mat
  - use left hand, right hand, together
  - walk hands along the floor – fast like a spider, then slow like a caterpillar

Peace at last

Use the space but stay close together

☐ Stretch neck, slowly let head fall until the chin is on the chest
  - I can relieve tension in my neck and shoulders

☐ Scrunch and let go!
  - I can be tense or relaxed and know the difference

☐ Sit quietly and listen to music – some classical music or 'healing' music
  - I can be peaceful

Session 5 - Explanations

Hello and welcome

Sitting in a circle

☐ Say your own name as you pass a teddy or soft toy
- Another inclusive game to develop a sense of belonging. Children may like to share their favourite soft toy or puppet.

☐ Ask children to *'Stand up if you… have hair that is brown/black/curly/ long, are the youngest in your family, are wearing blue socks, feel happy'.*

☐ Pass a frown around the circle. Then pass it the other way. Follow the frown by a smile. Then ask children to choose or mirror what is given by the previous child.

Getting going

Using the whole space of the hall or room

☐ Jump in and out of a hoop placed on the floor and repeat
- Ask children to perform the jump on their own or copy a friend moving round the hoop.

☐ Jump slowly, then jump fast: forwards, backwards, sideways.

☐ Cross-over: left hand to right knee, right hand to left knee, right hand to left foot raised behind, then left hand to right foot raised behind
- These actions cross the mid-line and are important to integrate both sides of the body.

☐ Single-sided: lower your right hand to meet your right knee, then lower your left hand to meet your left knee
- Actions here confine movements to each side of the body. Alternate with the cross-over.

Stop and pause

Using a more confined space

☐ Breathe in and lift hands in the air. Breathe out and slowly bring arms down to the floor.

☐ Awareness of fingers
- spread your fingers
- stretch and curl
- count fingers
- move fingers independently
- match fingers together, palm to palm
- match fingers with a partner's and touch one by one.

☐ Ankles
- sit with legs straight out in front, push toes away, pull toes in
- sit with legs straight out in front, let feet fall sideways outwards and come together
- sit with legs straight out in front, rotate left ankle, right ankle, together
- stand, rock from balls of feet to heels and back
- walk on the spot, heel first
- walk forward on toes, backwards on heels, eyes open, eyes closed.

☐ Thumbs
- thumb up, thumb down, left hand, right hand, together
- opposite thumbs up or down
- touch thumb to fingers one at a time using left hand, right hand, then together.

☐ Using fingers
- sit on the mat, use fingertips to roll a large ball round your mat
- use left hand, right hand, together

- walk hands along the floor –
  fast like a spider, then slow like
  a caterpillar.

Peace at last

Use the space but stay close together

- [ ] Stretch neck, slowly let head fall until the chin is on the chest.
    - Ask children to stretch gently without forcing any muscles. Keep the head and neck in alignment. Feel the muscles down the back.

- [ ] Scrunch and let go!
    - Sit or lie on the floor, eyes open or closed. Ask children to tense a group of muscles, hold that state of tension for a few seconds and then relax. For example, *'Clench your fist into a ball, hold for a count of five and then relax. Now scrunch all the parts of your face into a funny shape, hold and let go. Now tense the muscles in your bottom, hold and relax.'*

- [ ] Sit quietly and listen to music – some classical music or 'healing' music
    - Ask children to notice their breathing and how relaxed their muscles feel.

Session 6

Hello and welcome

Sitting in a circle

☐ Pass a mirror at the bottom of a box around the group saying, *'In the box is a picture of the most important person in the whole room. Don't say anything until everyone has seen who the person is'*
   - I know that I am someone special

☐ Go around the circle: *'Emma is clever because she can… tie her laces/ride a bike/run fast/find her coat peg'*
   - I can recognise something special about someone else

☐ Pass the ring
   - I am aware of others and can anticipate

Getting going

Using the whole space of the hall or room

☐ Hop on your left leg, then your right leg on the spot, forwards or backwards
   - I am able to balance

☐ Help a friend to hop by offering a hand to balance
   - I can be a good friend

☐ Take strides as big as possible

☐ Clap with a steady beat, slowly, quickly. Make a rhythm such as clap clap stop clap clap stop. Child copies partner
   - I can notice other people

☐ Jump forward two steps, backwards two steps, repeat

Stop and pause

Using the whole space of the hall or room

☐ Place weight on hands, bending body over, lift one leg, then the other. Keep hands still and make feet walk away from the body and then back again
   - I can make my body do as I say

☐ Shoulders
   - Lie on the floor, hands at side, sweep hands up and along the floor to meet above the head and clap
   - Lift arms over the head, down and sweep along the floor to sides
   - Stand, slowly rotate one shoulder, then the other, then together, forwards then backwards
   - Stand, arms out at sides, palms facing up, then down and repeat
   - Stand, swing right arm, left arm, together, opposite, encourage knees to bend as arms drop

☐ Throwing
   - Throw a bean bag anywhere onto the mat
   - Throw onto a cross on the mat
   - From one metre, two metres throw to a partner's mat
   - Throw a small ball into a box, then a large ball

☐ Catching
   - Sit with legs wide, catch a large ball rolled along the ground
   - Sit and catch a large ball thrown to you
   - Stand and catch a large ball, then a small ball
   - Catch a bean bag thrown to you
   - Catch with one hand
   - Bounce and catch a ball

Peace at last

Use the space but stay close together

- [ ] Stand, lift arms, make five big circles one way, then the other way, rotating from the shoulders. Start using quick rotations and then gradually slow down and stop
    - I can control and alter the speed of my movements

- [ ] Progressive muscle relaxation
    - I know how to calm myself down

Session 6 - Explanations

Hello and welcome

Sitting in a circle

☐ Pass a mirror at the bottom of a box around the group saying, *'In the box is a picture of the most important person in the whole room. Don't say anything until everyone has seen who the person is'* .

☐ Go around the circle: *'Emma is clever because she can…. tie her laces/ride a bike/run fast/find her coat peg'.*

☐ Pass the ring
   - Sit in a circle. Have a length of string that is long enough to reach round the circle, threaded through a ring and tied in a knot. One person starts by holding the ring that is then passed secretly from hand to hand, child to child, around the group.
   - Children will need to be aware of each other and look for signs to guess where the ring is. They will need to be able to anticipate the ring coming to them and be sensitive to touch.

Getting going

Using the whole space of the hall or room

☐ Hop on your left leg, then your right leg on the spot, forwards or backwards

☐ Help a friend to hop by offering a hand to balance
   - By now children should be used to working together and helping each other.

☐ Take strides as big as possible.

☐ Clap with a steady beat, slowly, quickly. Make a rhythm such as clap clap stop clap clap stop. Child copies partner.

☐ Jump forward two steps, backwards two steps, repeat
   - See how far children can jump. Set a target and see if this can be exceeded.

Stop and pause

Using the whole space of the hall or room

☐ Place weight on hands, bending body over, lift one leg, then the other. Keep hands still and make feet walk away from the body and then back again
   - Children may like to look at the shapes made by others or to photograph each other's shapes.

☐ Shoulders
   - Lie on the floor, hands at side, sweep hands up and along the floor to meet above the head and clap
   - Lift arms over the head, down and sweep along the floor to sides
   - Stand, slowly rotate one shoulder, then the other, then together, forwards then backwards
   - Stand, arms out at sides, palms facing up, then down and repeat
   - Stand, swing right arm, left arm, together, opposite, encourage knees to bend as arms drop

☐ Throwing
   - Throw a bean bag anywhere onto the mat
   - Throw onto a cross on the mat

- From one metre, two metres
- Throw to a partner's mat
- Throw a small ball into a box, then a large ball.

☐ Catching
- Sit with legs wide, catch a large ball rolled along the ground
- Sit and catch a large ball thrown to you
- Stand and catch a large ball then a small ball
- Catch a bean bag thrown to you
- Catch with one hand
- Bounce and catch a ball.

Peace at last

Use the space but stay close together

☐ Stand, lift arms, make five big circles one way, the other way, rotating from the shoulders. Start using quick rotations and then gradually slow down and stop.

☐ Progressive muscle relaxation
- Sit or lie comfortably on the floor, close your eyes. Ask children to relax the muscles of their body progressively as you guide them through. For example, *'Think about your face and make your eyes relax, make your mouth relax and your nose relax. Now think of your neck muscles and let go of any tension there. Let your shoulders sink down, then your arms and hands. Make your tummy relax and your back and bottom. Now think about your legs and make them feel heavy. Lastly, let your feet relax.'*
- You may like to test the state of relaxation by gently lifting a child's arm or leg to see if it will flop down in a relaxed way. Use this activity to unwind gradually, going from fast, tense actions to slow, smooth rotations, ready for the next activity. Use muscle relaxation to unwind gradually, to reach a calm and peaceful state.

Appendix A
Children's evaluation

Did you enjoy the sessions?　　　　Yes ☐　　　A bit ☐　　　No ☐

What did you like doing best?

Is there anything you did not like?

What do you think you have got better at?

At what other times do you do the movements?

How does this help you?

Anything else to say?

Appendix B
Parents' evaluation

What has your child said about the sessions?

What do you think your child enjoyed the most?

Is there anything your child did not like?

What do you think your child has got better at?

Have you noticed any other changes?

How do you think the sessions have helped?

Would you recommend the sessions for other children?

Any other comments?

Appendix C
Teachers' questionnaire
Use the prepared questions and add your own

Skills	Poor			Good	
	1	2	3	4	5
Is this child attentive when there are instructions or explanations in class?					
Can this child join in discussions?					
Can this child take turns?					
Does this child work well with others?					
Is this child good at following instructions?					
Does this child know how to calm him/herself?					
Can this child complete tasks independently?					
Is this child usually calm in class?					
Is this child good at sharing?					
Can this child use appropriate body language?					

Appendix D
Parents' questionnaire

Use the prepared questions and add your own

Skills	Poor			Good	
	1	2	3	4	5
Is your child attentive when there are instructions or explanations at home?					
Can your child join in discussions?					
Can your child take turns?					
Does your child work well with others?					
Is your child good at following instructions?					
Does your child know how to calm him/herself?					
Can your child complete activities independently?					
Is your child usually calm at home?					
Is your child good at sharing?					
Can your child use appropriate body language?					

References

Dennison, Paul (1989) *Brain Gym: Teacher's Edition*, Edu-Kinesthetics.

Morris, Elizabeth and Scott, Caroline (2002) *Emotional Literacy Indicators*, School of Emotional Literacy Publishing.

Palmer, Hap (2001) 'The Music, Movement and Learning Connection', *Young Children*, September.

Schneider, Ingun (2001) 'Balance, Posture, and Movement: Optimizing Children's Learning Capacities through Integration of the Sensory Motor System', *Renewal,* Spring/Summer.